*This Advent Book is dedicated
to my family and to the One whom together
we have celebrated and waited for every Christmas:
Jesus Christ.*

DEDICATION

ACKNOWLEDGEMENTS

Many thanks to the legion of advice givers, editors and proof-readers, especially Marty Kelly, Emily Bosh, Steve Hauge and Carissa Lewis. A million thanks goes to Hilary Horn for her fantastic photography and to Corinne Pingul for her graphic design and… so much more - she was a saint to work so long and so closely with me. And lastly, many thanks to our own three kids for their enthusiasm to celebrate and for their patience for my advent quirks. One more heart felt thanks to Carissa for her contagious holiday passion and to the many family members, neighbors and friends who joined us along the way to celebrate together.

To find out more information of how to order the younger children (up to 5 yr. old) or the older kids version, or to share ideas or feedback, please contact John at hongkong92@gmail.com.

ISBN: 978-0-9862456-0-2   Copyright 2014, all rights reserved.

"My family growing up made a special effort to celebrate the Christmas season together, so when I started my own family, I looked forward to shaping my own Advent traditions. John has been a close friend for years and I was eager to help him make his Advent book toddler friendly for my emerging family. After two years of working together, what you have before you is what our family does now each year with great enthusiasm. Enjoy!"
        —Emily Bosh

"John Lewis's Advent experience has equipped our young family to take the traditions and experiences of Christmas – that naturally make kids' eyes dance – and infuse them with meaning and opportunities for teachable moments even at the ages of 4 or 5. While there is more in this book than we will ever do in one Christmas season, I look forward to trying different combinations of activities/conversations as our kids grow and mature. This year I joyfully passed on several copies of the book to families I have met at my sons' public elementary school. In an ideal world, anyone who is training up their children in the Christian faith would appreciate this book."
        —Pam Wenz

Tips and Warnings from a veteran mom:

1. Start small. If you have never done much of this (family devotions, etc.), then try a few things and see how it goes. Remain flexible.

2. Take cues from your kids. If the exercise is not engaging, life-giving, helpful or fun, then don't push them. You may want to adapt or paraphrase or omit, but don't simply push your kids uphill because they are supposed to do this.

3. Beware of your own heart. If you are doing this because YOU are supposed to, that will bleed over to the kids. Your joy and energy are equally contagious and crucial for a good experience.

        —Teresa Silver

Over the years, Carissa and I identified hopes for our children during the Christmas season. These goals helped us create a framework for our family Advent book. And we both attended churches that celebrated the season of Advent. The Sunday after Thanksgiving began four weeks of lighting the Advent candle, carols and hearing a sermon series that led us to the crescendo of Christmas Eve.

As parents we wanted to build on our own previous experiences and create some new traditions of our own. We began with little steps when our first son Jonathan was one year old. By the time Ellie our first daughter was born, we had become first-hand witnesses of Christmas' magic: our kids opened up their hearts wide in this special and exciting season-why not point that magic toward the Christ child as much as possible?

We kept experimenting, led by Carissa's gift of making family memories special and holiday traditions joyful. By Rachel's arrival, we now could boast of our nativity players: young Joseph, pig- tailed Mary and six-week-old baby "Jesus." Several years later, I had developed an outline for our four weeks of celebrating advent with joy, fun and purpose and then kept experimenting with new ideas. I kept writing things down until this little book took shape.

We would never want to give the impression that we used this book rigidly or completely. Not at all! We flexed. Schedules, sickness, moods, spontaneity all impacted what we did day to day, if anything at all some days. But this book served as a MENU to choose from, a place to start, and a reminder that we would make room for what otherwise be sidelined altogether. As a dad, however, I so appreciated us having something I could use to take my leadership role in the home during this Christ centered season.

Here are three objectives that are behind our family Advent traditions and this book:

1. To appreciate more deeply the connections of the Christmas story with the Christmas symbols.

2. To have the Christmas season provide an annual revisiting of key foundations of our Christian faith.

3. To see these Christmas traditions prepare our children for a lifetime of making faith commitments in the real world.

(Note: First time users, please see the more detailed description of these three important goals in Appendix II at the back)

LEWIS FAMILY,
CHRISTMAS
1996

"Our family advent experience has always prepared my mind and heart for the Christmas season and the fact that Jesus was born for each of us."

—Jonathan

"Our family has celebrated advent together as long as I can remember. I love all the activities we do as a family from acting out the Adam and Eve story to watching Charlie Brown's classic video. The Christmas season would be very different without the advent traditions we do together."

—Ellie

"Many of my most treasured Christmas memories have had something do with this advent book: to a kid, what could be better than getting to turn the "Light of the world" on and off when I plugged in the Christmas tree? Our family advent experience never fails to remind me of what we are truly celebrating and has developed a close relationship between my Savior and I during the Christmas season."

—Rachel

TABLE OF CONTENTS

WEEK ONE

JESUS IS THE TREE OF LIFE AND LIGHT OF THE WORLD

❧SYMBOLS - THE TREE AND THE LIGHTS

SUNDAY: Jesus is the Tree of Life and the Light of the World

MONDAY: God Creates the World with Life and Light

TUESDAY: Adam and Eve Disobeyed God and Darkness Returned

WEDNESDAY: God Gives His Disobedient People a Promise for Light and Life

THURSDAY: A Baby Boy and a Baby Church Bring Light and Life

FRIDAY: We Today Bring Light and Life to the World.

SATURDAY: Heaven Will be Full of Jesus and His Light and Life

WEEK TWO

JESUS CAME TO THE EARTH LIKE ONE OF US

❧SYMBOLS - ORNAMENTS AND NATIVITY SET

SUNDAY: Jesus Came to Earth Like One of Us

MONDAY: Jesus Came as a Human Being

TUESDAY: Jesus was Born in a Special Family

WEDNESDAY: Jesus was Born in a Special Place

THURSDAY: Jesus was Born at a Special Time

FRIDAY: Jesus was Born a Hebrew

SATURDAY: Jesus was Born in Poverty

WEEK THREE

WE GIVE BECAUSE GOD FIRST GAVE JESUS

❧SYMBOLS - GIFTS AND STOCKINGS

SUNDAY: We Give Because God First Gave Jesus to Us

MONDAY: Jesus Came to Us as a Surprise from God

TUESDAY: Thanks and Praise are My Gift to God

WEDNESDAY: It's a Gift When We Say YES

THURSDAY: God Gave Jesus Like Santa Gives Gifts

FRIDAY: Jesus Came as a Sheperd to Make a Sacrifice

SATURDAY: God Gave Us Gifts to Share with Others

WEEK FOUR

STARS AND ANGELS POINT THE WAY TO JESUS

❧SYMBOLS - STAR AND ANGELS

SUNDAY: Stars and Angels Point the Way to Jesus

MONDAY: Jesus is the Brightest Star of All

TUESDAY: Everyone Needs a Star

WEDNESDAY: The Magi Followed the Star by Night

THURSDAY: The Angel Pointed to the Future

FRIDAY: The Star Pointed to a Greater Christmas

CHRISTMAS EVE! THE WAITING IS OVER, JESUS IS HERE!

INTRODUCING ADVENT

"But Mary treasured all these words and pondered them in her heart." Luke 2:19

Advent is the four-week season before Christmas set aside for remembering "the Coming" (Advent's literal meaning) of Jesus first into our world as a human and some day as reigning King. But sometimes the holiday hustle can make us feel just like those who missed the first coming of baby Jesus. What should be so central seems the thing most easily overlooked. For followers of Jesus, our intentional "remembering" is perhaps the most important part of "getting ready for Christmas."

Our first model of remembering Christ's birth is Mary, Jesus' mother. On this birth night, she is said to have "treasured all these things in her heart." Undoubtedly she held dear the memories all mothers do about her own new little one, but that cannot be all. She treasured the truth about this unique baby: the miraculous visit from an angel, the divine conception, the leaping in her cousin Elizabeth's womb, the angels heralding heaven's hymns to the shepherds in the night field, the Magi dumbstruck by a star they could not help but follow.

These details and their possible meaning would not escape her memory. Everything is remembered and tucked into her enduring imagination. Mary was wise to remember and ponder and treasure these memories in her heart. What mother is not glad for writing down some of the mannerisms and magical moments with her own child?

In the hailstorm of laundry and diapers, in the torrential current of paying bills and nagging interruptions, aren't we all easily distracted from the treasures of life? For me, this is never truer than during the Holidays and all the latent meaning held within the Christmas story and symbols. Unburying the treasure in Christmas demands our attention, too. So traditions of remembering become a true gift indeed.

In the spirit of Mary, Advent invites us to set aside moments to ponder and treasure this mystery in our own hearts. And while it may have come naturally to Mary, for most of us living in today's world, a more sustained effort is required. Beginning and protecting family traditions at Christmas can spur us on to what we deep down really long for as a family.

Studies over the years have shown that families who practice traditions bond together more deeply and foster security among all its members. For Christians, the stakes of developing Christ-centered traditions run even higher: what kind of faith will our kids practice when they leave our home and start their own families? Most likely their daily walk of faith will imitate their home life more than their church life. Our faith does not automatically transfer to our kids; strong competitors for their loyalty ambush our children the moment they leave our home, and even when they live within it. So Advent for Carissa and I has not only been a priority for seeing Christ in Christmas but an opportunity and season for much, much more. The Jewish people passed on their faith to the next generation by using stories and traditions; we, too, wanted during the holiday season to have our own yearly traditions help cement faith in our children. Advent has been one of our most potent experiences.

Christmas traditions help shape our children's hearts, enrich our family's faith, and prepare us to be Christ's salt and light in a world that has largely forgotten the Jesus story.

While Jesus is unforgettably wonderful, the meaning of Christmas must be persistently remembered.

INTRODUCING THE BASICS OF THE BOOK

WHO: this version of the Advent book is targeted for families with toddlers and young children; it also could be easily used or adapted for Christian preschools, kindergartens, and Sunday school classes. (Note: a companion version is also available for families with elementary to high school-aged kids).

WHEN: We begin on the first Sunday of Advent and end on Christmas Eve. Sundays are traditionally the best day to anchor Advent in your home. On each Sunday page you will find needed resources you may need, introductions for the week, and about twenty minutes of age-appropriate and theme-related activities. Weekdays get busier, so we offer here ten to fifteen minutes of theme related activities for the other days of the week.

WHAT: This Advent book was created to develop long-term traditions and memories that could grow up and flex with all the changes that our family experienced. *It is intended for all who use it to be a MENU to choose from not a workbook to complete or feel guilty.* Though it's not required, we recommend you consider using it this way. Year after year we returned to the basics of the Christian Christmas story.

Week One: The *tree* and the *lights* throughout the bigger salvation story of the Bible. We start on Monday in the Creation story, move through the Fall, Old Testament, Jesus and the church of the New Testament and then the church today: us! Saturday ends with the final coming of Christ. This larger story is our first foundation of faith and of Christmas.

Week Two: *Ornaments* and the *Nativity scene* help emphasize the pervasive presence of Jesus. This is the essence of the Incarnation-a crucial Christian tenet: Christ was then, and is now, Emmanuel, God present to us in the ordinary and even troublesome experiences of our human life on earth.

Week Three: *Gifts* and *Stockings* (and their origin, the Saint Nicholas story) remind us that we give generously as a response to first receiving what we did not deserve. "We love because He first loved us" (1 John 4:19) is the basic rhythm behind not only our shopping and wrapping, but also behind the entire life of following Jesus.

Week Four: The *Star* and *Angels* point us to the truth that mankind dwells naturally in darkness but also seeks God's light of truth to guide us in our life journey. We are followers, not leaders, disciples not masters, sheep not shepherd-and Jesus goes ahead of His sheep as the star went ahead of the magi.

Each day for each week you will find different combinations of five of the following (remember: you can freely choose to do some, none, or all):

- *A scripture to look up and read out loud:* use a kid friendly adult Bible and ideally you would also have access to a good children's Bible-The Jesus Storybook Bible, e.g. To get our kids more involved in the Christmas story, we sometimes drew them in by acting out the story, or had them repeat out loud some of what we read to them.

- *A short activity to engage in.* Any materials that are needed are noted at the beginning of the page.

- *Something to discuss:* parents take the lead and, if need be, adapt to kids' capacity or context.

- *A memory verse to review:* one short verse related to the week's theme, which can be written and posted in the house as well.

- *A Christmas carol to sing:* words are found in Appendix III at the back of the book.

- *A final short prayer:* one prayer for the week, the same each day. An adult can pray it alone, or read it line by line and ask the kids to repeat.

- *Optional video to watch:* On Sunday, one or two classic Christmas viewing options related to the week's themes are suggested. It can be viewed on Sunday itself after the advent time, or some other time that week. We have loved doing this as a family.

STARTING TIPS:

Plan ahead: Schedules and seasons of life led us to experiment in a variety of ways. We gathered at the beginning of each Advent and then even each week to put this agreed time into our schedule. The amount of time available helped dictate how many of the activities we would do.

Sundays: Procure and decorate an Advent wreath and candle ahead of time; it will likely be an anchor of your Advent memories. Our family puts up the two weekly Christmas symbols each Sunday; by not putting up all eight symbols all at once we found it easier to highlight each one, and we were as well invited to be patient and to wait, which of course is at the heart of Advent.

Week One Extra: Our family's tradition is to go to a tree farm the Saturday of Thanksgiving weekend, just before the start of Advent. It is not only fun but is full of potential symbolism (Jesus was "cut off" and came from "heaven's tree farm" to be in our home and "living room," e.g.). You will find just before Week One a short reflection and then a poem from our daughter Rachel to use on such a pre-advent occasion.

The Uniqueness of Week Four: The number of days for the last week of Advent varies, depending on what day Christmas falls. Week Four always starts off with Sunday, and always has a Christmas Eve day experience. All other days are available with resources.

PRAYER:

"Father God, may the inexhaustible simplicity of Christ's birth warm our hearts again this Christmas season. Help us to celebrate this season as if we were having a birthday party, and so much more, because… we are. Let the mysteries of your son Jesus coming with skin on awaken in us deeper awe. May our Advent experience help enrich our faith and hope in You. Let the Christmas message hold us in her wonder all year long. Amen."

GETTING YOUR CHRISTMAS TREE

JESUS LEAVES HIS NATURAL HOME TO LIVE WITH US ON EARTH

These are options for you and your family to use on the day you jump in your car to go cut, purchase and then put up your Christmas tree.

THINGS TO DO:

BEFORE GETTING THE TREE –

REFLECTION: The heart, and the start of Christmas, was God's decision to send his Son to earth to be among us. It wasn't natural for Jesus to leave home and become a human being on the speck of dust we call earth. In fact, it was costly for Jesus to come to us and be like us in a way natural for us. So the day we get our Christmas tree – even fake ones – can point us to this first Christmas truth: Trees are each holiday season cut down and emptied, taken from their natural place of dirt and forest. This "death" allows us to behold their beauty and fragrance in the familiarity of our own home and hearth. It's easy to take it for granted but the tree gave its life in order for it to be with us.

VIII

AFTER THE TREE IS UP –

READ Philippians 2:5-7

DISCUSS: Why is it not natural for a tree to be in our living room? Why was it not easy or natural for Jesus to leave heaven come to earth and "plant" Himself among us? What did He have to give up? *Read* the poem, "I Give my Life" by Rachel Lewis when she was 15.

PRAY "Oh Lord, It's so very beautiful but it is not natural for this tree to be in this room. So, too, it was not natural for you to be "cut off" from heaven and your Father's presence. . . but we are so glad you did. Your beauty in the middle of our living room, of our home and heart was made possible because you came as one of us. We are glad you did! Thank you so much."

I GIVE MY LIFE
BY RACHEL LEWIS

I am tall and proud
I am a ladder that can't be climbed
I reach up to the heavens
I am beautiful.

I dance in the wind
I sing in the rain
I smile in the sun
I sigh in the snow.

They come together
They glance, their furrowed frowns
Sunny smiles, ringing laugh
Fingers of rain touch me.

Standing like a tower
Seeing sharp clawed hands
Pleading to live
Gasping for breath.

Leaving everything,
My comforting home below
Fresh breath around me
My own little heaven.

Desperately dying
Snapping limbs
Pain shooting up my now withering body
Yet the laughter inside keeps me living.

Twisted, turning, down, down
Lifted, carried, balanced
Rest at last covers me like a soft blanket
A drink like a cool mountain spring.

Small tender hands upon me
And mellow sleepy lights
Oohs and Ahs like a soft sweet song
Carrying precious gifts upon me.

Loved at last
Like none but me
My death worth it
I would do it all again.

LEWIS FAMILY AND CHRISTMAS TREE, 2013

WEEK ONE

JESUS IS THE TREE OF LIFE
AND THE LIGHT OF THE WORLD

THIS WEEK'S EMPHASIS IS
following the Bible story from its beginning to its middle and to its end, using the symbols of trees and lights along the way.

Christmas symbols to set out together: tree, lights on tree or house, wreath, Advent candle and wreath.

Additional Resources: "Charlie Brown Christmas" movie, paper, washable markers, crayons, red ball ornaments, a picture of a baby that you know, flashlights.

Connecting to your Neighborhood (can be done anytime during the week): Once it is dark, go on a short neighborhood walk together as a family, even if the weather is not good. Enjoy the Christmas lights. Let the kids hold the flashlights as a sign that we are God's light. Pray for your neighbors by name or stop by a house and sing a carol.

SUNDAY

JESUS AS THE TREE OF LIFE AND THE LIGHT OF THE WORLD

Trees and their green branches are symbols of life at Christmas. They remind us that God created the world and all the living things. Jesus is also alive inside our hearts.

Lights are also symbols at Christmas. God created light so that we could see. God created Jesus to be a light to the world to help people see God's love. God calls us to be a light to the world too.

Additional Resources: Tree, lights, Bible, Advent candle/wreath, Charlie Brown Christmas movie

THINGS TO DO:

READ John 1:4-5 – notice the words ***light*** and ***life*** (Matt 1:22 is this week's memory verse option: "A teenage girl shall conceive and bear a son and you shall call His name, Emmanuel, which means, 'God with us.'").

PUT UP the tree and its lights.

LIGHT the Advent candle. This week it is the candle of Prophecy. Optional: Put greens around the Advent Candle. Read: Isaiah 9:2 and 11:1-2 as you first light and then look at the candle.

SING "O Come All Ye Faithful" and begin to memorize together Matt .1:21: "A teenage girl shall conceive and bear a son and you shall call His name, Emmanuel, which means, 'God with us.'"

PRAY "Thank you God for creating me and the world in which I live. Thank you for making my heart clean again when I disobey, mess up and make my heart dirty. Help me learn about all the ways you have loved people so that I can do my important job of loving people like Jesus did."

WATCH: Today, or later this week – watch the classic ***A Charlie Brown Christmas*** movie. (Notice how Jesus is like the little green tree: See: http://www.youtube.com/watch?v=JQeKdvXliIU)

3

Monday

God Creates the World with Life and Light

At the beginning of God's story, God created life on earth and light for us to see. These are precious gifts that came when God created the world. He still gives us Life and Light!

Additional Resources: Bible/children's Bible, paper and markers, crayons or pens

Things to Do:

READ the Creation story of Genesis 1 from a children's Bible or tell it yourself in a way kids can understand.

DRAW as a whole family together or individually, one or two things God created in the beginning, then share with each other.

ASK What would happen to these things God created if there was no longer any light in the world? Then put your fingers over everything you drew that would no longer exist.

REVIEW the memory verse- Matt 1:21 "A teenage girl shall conceive and bear a son and you shall call His name, Emmanuel, which means, 'God with us.'"

SING "Silent Night" v. 2.

PRAY "Thank you God for making me and the world I live in so beautiful. Thank you for making my heart clean again when I disobey you. Help me learn about all the ways you have loved people so that I can do my important job of loving others like Jesus did."

TUESDAY

ADAM AND EVE DISOBEYED GOD AND DARKNESS RETURNED

The beginning of our story continued with Adam and Eve disobeying God. God was still with them, though they were surrounded by darkness. We, too, disobey God and also can feel lost and afraid when we are in the dark. That's why Jesus will come later in our story, to bring us light and make us alive again.

Additional Resources: Red ball ornament, flashlight

THINGS TO DO:

TURN OUT all the house and Christmas lights, close the curtains and sit a moment in the dark. Explain that sin, or disobeying God, also makes us feel lost in the dark.

READ the story of "The Fall" (Genesis 3:1-7) in the dark with a children's or a regular Bible using a flashlight. Ask: What did Adam and Eve do that displeased God? Why did they disobey? What happened to Adam and Eve after they disobeyed? Do we sometimes do the same kind of thing that Adam and Eve did? (Parents share an example first)

TURN ON the lights and be thankful Jesus does not leave us in our sin and darkness! Then, as a traditional symbol of our own sins, put a round, plain red ornament on the tree.

REVIEW the memory verse: Matt 1:21 "A teenage girl shall conceive and bear a son and you shall call His name, Emmanuel, which means, 'God with us.'"

PRAY "Thank you God for creating me and the world I live in so beautiful. Thank you for making my heart clean again when I disobey you. Help me learn about all the ways you have loved people so that I can do my important job of loving others like Jesus did."

5

WEDNESDAY

GOD GIVES HIS DISOBEDIENT PEOPLE A PROMISE FOR LIGHT AND LIFE

God's plan to save us after the Garden of Eden started with Abraham and included men like Moses and David, women like Ruth and Esther, and many other special leaders. His special people, Israel, and their leaders did not always love God or each other, nor did they always obey His commands. Still, God gave them a promise to make all things good in the future by one day sending us His Son.

Additional Resource: Several red ball ornaments

THINGS TO DO:

REMEMBER the people of the Old Testament also sinned like Adam and Eve. Play charades or recall one or two specific stories in the Old Testament where sins were committed by individuals and by the Israeli people as a whole.

PUT red balls on the Christmas tree as symbols of the sins of Israel in the Old Testament.

READ two Old Testament promises about the Messiah that include the symbol of a tree and light: Isaiah 49:6b and Jeremiah 33:15-16. Can you see how Jesus made them both come true?

SING "O Come, O Come Emmanuel" v. 1 and imagine Israel in the Old Testament singing this song.

PRAY "Thank you God for creating me and the world I live in so beautiful. Thank you for making my heart clean again when I disobey you. Help me learn about all the ways you have loved people so that I can do my important job of loving others like Jesus did."

THURSDAY

A BABY JESUS AND A BABY CHURCH BRING LIGHT AND LIFE

In the middle of God's Big Story, Jesus came into the world as a baby, a real person just like you and me. He came, however, with an important job to do. He came as the Light and Life to save us from darkness, to clean us where we are dirty and then live inside us.

Additional Resources: Picture of a baby you know, nativity set

THINGS TO DO:

REVIEW the Memory verse: Matt 1:21 - "A teenage girl shall conceive and bear a son and you shall call His name, Emmanuel, which means, 'God with us.'"

READ Luke 2:1-7 or tell this story on your own as the parent, or tell it together in your own words as a family.

ASK: What do you imagine the life of a shepherd was like in those days? Or of a young mother willing to give birth to the Messiah? In what way was Jesus' life like theirs?

SING "O Holy Night," v. 1.

PRAY "Thank you God for creating me and the world I live in so beautiful. Thank you for making my heart clean again when I disobey you. Help me learn about all the ways you have loved people so that I can do my important job of loving others like Jesus did."

FRIDAY

WE THE CHURCH ARE TO BRING HIS LIGHT AND LIFE TO THE WORLD

Today, 2000 years after Jesus first came, His Spirit lives in us and has made us His forever family. He then shared His important job with His new Baby Church. And we have the same important job that the shepherds, Jesus and the Baby Church had: we are to bring His Light and Life to the world!

Additional Resources: Flashlights

THINGS TO DO:

READ Luke 2: 16-18. The story of the Shepherds sharing their news with others who had not seen "the Light."

READ Matthew 5:14-16. What is something our family did this year that helped others see the Light of Jesus?

SHARE in the story it was the shepherd's important job to show others that Jesus is the Life and Light of the world. They proclaimed it to their friends. Who in our life needs to see who Jesus is? How can we today in a similar way to the Shepherds do our important job of telling others about Jesus in a good way?

ACTIVITY: after dark, go on a short neighborhood walk together as a family. Enjoy the Christmas lights and think of Jesus. Let the kids hold the flashlights as a sign that we are together God's light. Pray for your neighbors. Stop in on one, wish them a Merry Christmas.

PRAY "Thank you God for living in me and calling me to join you in being the Light of the world with my family. Help me learn about all the ways you have loved people so that I can do my important job of showing them love and telling others about Jesus."

8

SATURDAY

HEAVEN WILL BE FULL OF JESUS AND HIS LIFE AND LIGHT

At the end of God's great and true story, Jesus will come back again, not as a baby or a human but as an amazing King, full of Life and Light. And when Jesus does come back, heaven will come to earth and it will be incredible!

Additional Resources: White board or a large piece of paper, markers or crayons

THINGS TO DO:

READ Revelation 22:1-5. As you hear these words, close your eyes and use your imagination, or just listen to these words as you look at the tree and lights. What do these words from Revelation tell us God and Jesus will be like in heaven? What will life be like for us?

DRAW as a group out several things that Revelation 22:1-5 says about heaven using a white board or a large piece of paper. Remember together that the same God who promised Jesus to come the first time promised He would surely come again.

SING "Joy to the World," all the verses. Notice how much of this song is more relevant to Jesus' second coming as triumphant King than His first coming as a baby.

REVIEW the Memory Verse: Matt 1:21 "A teenage girl shall conceive and bear a son and you shall call His name, Emmanuel, which means, 'God with us.'"

PRAY "Thank you God for creating me and the world I live in so beautiful, and for the promise that heaven will be amazing. May the hope of heaven help inspire me to do my important job of loving others like Jesus did."

WEEK TWO

JESUS CAME TO EARTH
LIKE ONE OF US

THIS WEEK'S EMPHASIS IS

on the many particular ways Jesus came to dwell among us as a human and as a poor baby, in Bethlehem. This week you might want everyone to look at the tree ornaments or the nativity set as you read the scriptures or sing the carols.

Christmas Symbols to set out together: Nativity set and ornaments for the Christmas tree.

Additional Resources: Advent wreath and candles, children Bible's story about the birth of Jesus, family photo albums or computer pictures of your children and family, new ornament for this year or materials to make one, globe or world map.

Connecting to your Neighborhood, Community and World: Pray for particular groups of people suffering in your own city, then in your country and then for countries suffering most in the world. You can use a globe or world map to point out the designated countries. End by thanking God in a short prayer for Jesus becoming poor that we would not die but become rich in Him.

SUNDAY

JESUS CAME TO EARTH LIKE ONE OF US

God came to us in baby Jesus as someone just like us. Our ornaments and nativity set remind us that Jesus, like us, had a story of being born, a special family, a special birthplace. Jesus was in so many ways just like us!

Additional Resources: Ornaments, Nativity set, Advent candle

THINGS TO DO:

PUT UP some of your favorite tree ornaments, sharing as you do stories about them. If you have one, set up your nativity set except for baby Jesus; place him aside for next week. Gather around and identify all the nativity characters of the story. What job or role did each of them have in the birth story of Jesus?

LIGHT the first candle from last week, then light the Bethlehem Advent candle and *pray*, "Dear Jesus, thank you for coming as a baby to do your important job of saving us. Help me to understand more about the life you came to live. Remind me through the ornaments and the nativity set that you and I were both born to a special family, in a special place, at a special time."

READ the story of "The Farmer and the Birds" by Paul Harvey (find this online)

SING "Away in the Manger," v. 1

WATCH the *Frosty the Snowman* video (note the scene where Frosty became...like one of us: see http://www.youtube.com/watch?v=yDiyKU8H4-)

13

Monday

Jesus Came as a Baby

People love babies and get really excited when they are around them. God wants us and the whole world to be excited about Baby Jesus!

Things to Do:

READ Isaiah 9:6: "…Unto us a child is born, unto us a Son is given."

SHOW everyone a picture of a baby you all know, and then ask: what do most babies do that make people like them? Why do you like babies? Do you think Jesus was just like the babies you know?

ASK, after showing everyone a picture of a baby you all know: Why do you like babies? What do they sound like and look like? What do they do? How do you think Jesus was just like the babies you know?

ASK, since God sent Jesus as a Baby King, do you think He got the same kind of attention most babies get? How do you think God wants people to pay attention to the baby Jesus at Christmas?

REVIEW the Memory Verse: John 1:14 – "God came in human flesh and moved into our neighborhood."

PRAY "Dear Jesus, thank you for coming as a baby to do your important job of saving us. Help me to understand more about the life you came to live. Remind me through the ornaments and the nativity set that you and I both were born to a special family, in a special place, at a special time."

TUESDAY
JESUS IS BORN IN A SPECIAL FAMILY

Just like you are part of a special family, Jesus was part of a special family.

Additional Resources: Photo album or computer with pictures of your children and family members

THINGS TO DO:

READ Luke 1:26-27 and as you, listen for the names of some of Jesus' biological family. Notice they were ordinary people in many ways. Then read Mark 3:35 and see who else Jesus said was part of His "extended" family.

LOOK and find some pictures of the people you consider to be part of your biological and "extended" family. The pictures can be these people all by themselves or even better, with your family member(s) in the picture.

ASK: What are the names of all the people in God's special family He made for you? Name them. What have they done for you or with you? Why are they important to you?

REVIEW the Memory Verse: John 1:14- "God came in human flesh and moved into our neighborhood."

PRAY "Dear Jesus, thank you for coming as a baby to do your important job of saving us. Help me to understand more about the life you came to live. Remind me through the ornaments and the nativity set that you and I both were born to be part of a special family, in a special place, at a special time."

WEDNESDAY

JESUS WAS BORN IN A SPECIAL PLACE

Ornaments can come from special places. They can remind us that Baby Jesus also was born in a special place.

Additional Resources: Ornament(s) from a particular place or memory

THINGS TO DO:

READ Luke 2:1-7 as you gather around the Nativity set.

DISCUSS: Where was the special setting and special place Jesus was born? In the country? Was it a big or a little place? In a hospital or in a house?

PUT UP some new and old ornaments that come from special places: vacation, road trip, previous home, etc.). Remember together what makes those places special, or remember together a special place your family visited this last year.

SING "O Little Town of Bethlehem," v. 1.

PRAY "Dear Jesus, thank you for coming as a baby to do your important job of saving us. Help me to understand more about the life you came to live. Remind me through the ornaments and the Nativity set that you and I were born into a special family, in a special place, at a special time."

THURSDAY
JESUS WAS BORN AT A SPECIAL TIME

God chose a special time to send Baby Jesus to the earth to live among people. And because He still lives among us today, our time here on earth is also special to Jesus-and to us!

Additional Resources: An ornament purchased earlier in the year, or materials to make a new one, calendar

THINGS TO DO:

SHARE with your kids some specific examples of things that have changed or been invented since you grew up as a child: (computers, phones, videogames, books, toys, cars, trains, bigger cities, grocery stores, population and pollution, etc.). We live today in a unique and special time!

REVIEW the Memory Verse: John 1:14- "God came in human flesh and moved into our neighborhood." He was present back then and is present today, through all the times and changes!

USE your calendar and your memory, and remember some special memories or events this year together. Re-tell a few of the stories briefly together. In what way was this year a special time for us?

MAKE or start to make, or buy, an ornament for your family that represents something special that happened this year for you.

PRAY "Dear Jesus, thank you for coming as a baby to do your important job of saving us. Help me to understand more about the life you came to live. Remind me through the ornaments and the Nativity set that you and I both were born to a special family, in a special place, at a special time."

FRIDAY

JESUS WAS BORN A HEBREW

While God is invisible, Jesus came as God in a human body, and not just any body, but the body of a Hebrew man. He looked like all his Jewish neighbors.

Additional Resource: Internet

THINGS TO DO:

FIND on the Internet a picture or two of a Palestinian man and then imagine Jesus with these Middle Eastern and Hebrew features.

FIND on the Internet a few images of Jesus and notice how these portraits of Jesus are different to the Palestinian photo you found. Why do we think Jesus is often painted to look like the ones who paint Him?

REVIEW the Memory Verse: John 1:14- "God came in human flesh and moved into our neighborhood."

SING "O come all ye faithful," vv. 1-2.

PRAY "Dear Jesus, thank you for coming as a baby to do your important job of saving us. Help me to understand more about the life you came to live. Remind me through the ornaments and the Nativity set this year that you and I were both born to a special family, in a special place, at a special time."

SATURDAY

JESUS WAS BORN IN POVERTY

Jesus was rich in heaven, but He was poor while He lived on earth.

Additional Resources: A globe or world map

READ 2 Corinthians 8:9: "Jesus became poor that we might become rich."

REMEMBER specifically how Jesus and his parents were poor and simple in his birth story, and also His childhood and ministry: Jesus was born not in a normal house but in a carved-out stone animal stable in the Bethlehem mountainside. He first had to flee with his family to Egypt; He later grew up in a small village and a very small house. Jesus' family had no money in the bank and was forced to pay a very big tax to the Romans. Jesus as an adult lived without having a house or a bank account; He traveled from town to town in His ministry years with only the clothes on His back. Can you see why poor people might find it easy to relate to Jesus?

REVIEW the memory verse: John 1:14- "God came in human flesh and moved into our neighborhood." Jesus moved into our poor world and became friends with poor people.

SING "Away in a Manger," v. 2.

PRAY for particular groups of poor and vulnerable people first in our own city, then in our country and then for countries suffering most in the world. You can use a globe, map or a few statistics to point out who and for what you are praying. End by thanking God in a short prayer for teaching us about how He loved the poor enough to come and live like them.

WEEK THREE

WE GIVE BECAUSE
GOD GAVE JESUS TO US

THIS WEEK'S EMPHASIS IS

focused on the theme of giving and receiving throughout the Christmas story. This week you may want everyone to look at the gifts under your tree or stockings as you read the scriptures or sing the carols.

Christmas Symbols to set out together: wrapped gifts and the stockings.

Additional Resources: Advent wreath and candles, gift wrapping supplies, Baby Jesus from Nativity set, candy canes, hot cocoa. Veggie Tales movie:"The Toy that Saved Christmas." Christmas classic: "The Drummer Boy."

Connecting to your Neighborhood, Community or World: Have each person make a coupon for someone you love outside your family (a neighbor, teacher or friend) where you give something of yourself for Christmas, such as a plate of cookies to a shut-in, a walk with a neighbor or assistance with a difficult chore.

SUNDAY

WE GIVE BECAUSE GOD FIRST GAVE JESUS TO US

When we receive the gift of Jesus from God, we naturally want to give gifts to others. Gifts remind us that the greatest gift we can receive is Jesus. Stockings remind us to give in the same spirit as St. Nicholas, who gave to people in need and without needing to be thanked.

Additional Resources: A few wrapped gifts, stockings, Advent wreath and candle

THINGS TO DO:

SET UP your stockings and set out some gifts under the tree together.

LIGHT the candle from previous weeks, then light the Advent Candle (Shepherd Candle). *Read* Luke 2: 8-12, 15-18 and notice how the shepherds both receive a gift and then give a gift: the gift of Good News. What was the gift the shepherds first received and then later that night shared with other people?

SING "Angels We Have Heard on High," v. 1

REVIEW Memory Verse: John 3:16 – "For God so loved the world that He gave His only Son that everyone who believes in Him should not perish but have everlasting life."

PRAY "Thank you, God, for the Greatest Gift ever given, Jesus your Son. Thank you for Baby Jesus who came to give us life and save us. As we learn more about the gift of your son Jesus, help us to give our greatest gifts to you, and to the people you want us to love."

WATCH one of these classic Christmas movies:

Veggie Tales: The Toy that Saved Christmas (Christmas is not about getting but about giving, as God gave Jesus)

The Drummer Boy (giving the gift of himself to the baby Jesus: last scene-youtube.com/watch?v=MDETOAHJj1c).

MONDAY

JESUS CAME TO US AS A SURPRISE FROM GOD

No one was expecting Jesus to come to earth, and when He came, He came like our Christmas gifts: He was wrapped up!

Additional Resources: Wrapping paper, scissors and tape, baby Jesus from Nativity set

THINGS TO DO:

READ Luke 2:6-7, the story of Baby Jesus wrapped in swaddling clothes, the first "wrapped" Christmas gift ever.

IMAGINE what Christmas would be like if our gifts under the tree did not have wrapping on them? How would Christmas morning be different?

PUT the baby Jesus from the Nativity set into a small box, wrap and then put Him under the tree OR wrap a gift together for someone outside of your family, and put it under the tree.

SING a favorite Christmas carol.

PRAY "Thank you, God, for the Greatest Gift ever given, Jesus your Son. Thank you for Baby Jesus who came to give us life and save us. As we learn more about the gift of your son Jesus, help us to give our greatest gifts to you, and to the people you want us to love."

TUESDAY

THANKS AND PRAISE ARE MY GIFT TO GOD

Being grateful involves thanking God for what God gives to us. God's heart is filled with gladness when we express our thanks to Him.

THINGS TO DO:

READ Luke 1:46-49. This is Mary giving thanks to God after she found out she was pregnant with Baby Jesus. When we, like Mary, thank God for what He did for us and who He is, God is as happy as we are.

REMEMBER a time someone thanked you or said something nice about you. How did that make you feel? That's how God feels when we thank and praise Him.

SIT in a circle and then share one thing you are specifically thankful for about the person on your left.

REVIEW Memory Verse: John 3:16 – "For God so loved the world that He gave His only Son that everyone who believes in Him should not perish but have everlasting life."

PRAY Have each person thank God for something that He has given to us in our everyday life. Have one parent make a list of these and then clip it onto the Christmas tree.

WEDNESDAY
IT'S A GIFT WHEN WE SAY YES TO GOD

When God in heaven asked Jesus to do His important job on earth, Jesus said "YES." When the angel asked Mary to do her important job of being Jesus' mother, Mary said "YES." It's a gift to God when we say YES to what He asks us to do, too.

Additional Resources: Wrapping paper, tape and small box

THINGS TO DO:

READ Luke 10:30-38, the story of Mary's visit by the angel where she says YES to God and His plan for her to be Jesus' mommy.

ASK: What was the important job the angel was asking Mary to do? Why might have it been hard for Mary to say YES to God's job for her?

SHARE: *Kids:* can you think of a recent example when you asked Mom or Dad to do something for you and then they smiled, said YES and did what you asked? How did that make you feel? *Parents:* How does it make you feel when your kids respond with a cheerful YES to what you ask?

WRITE the words "YES Lord" on a small cut piece of colored paper, have everyone sign it, then wrap it up in a box and put it under a tree as the gift of our family's willlingness to say YES to God this Christmas.

REVIEW the memory verse: John 3:16 "For God so loved the world that He gave His only Son that everyone who believes in Him should not perish but have everlasting life."

PRAY "Thank you, God, for the Greatest Gift ever given, Jesus your Son. Thank you for Baby Jesus who said YES to you and then came to give us life and save us. As we learn more about the gift of your son Jesus, help us to give our greatest gifts to you, and to the people you want us to love."

THURSDAY
GOD GAVE US JESUS LIKE SANTA GIVES US GIFTS

God gave Jesus without expecting us to give Him something back. This is how St. Nicholas first gave his gifts. We, too, are to give gifts with no strings attached.

Additional Resources: A Christmas baked good to share, a longer version of the St. Nicholas story in book or on the Web

THINGS TO DO:

READ the story behind Santa Claus: the story of Santa Claus comes from the legend of St. Nicholas, a bishop from centuries ago who deeply loved God and people. He became famous for sneaking into homes at night to put gifts in the socks of poor children that were hanging near the hearth to dry. His story has since captured the heart of the world, and nearly every nation has some kind of tradition around giving surprises to children on Christmas Eve. St. Nicholas freely received from Christ, so freely he gave.

READ Matthew 10:8-"Freely you have received; freely give." This verse is at the heart of today's theme: God gave Jesus freely. The original Santa Claus gave his gifts in response... and so do we.

REVIEW the memory verse: John 3:16 "For God so loved the world that He gave His only Son that everyone who believes in Him should not perish but have everlasting life."

SHARE a Christmas sweet with someone not expecting it, or do a secret act of service or kindness for someone in your neighborhood.

PRAY "Thank you, God, for the Greatest Gift ever given, Jesus your Son. Thank you for Baby Jesus who came to us freely with no demands that we give Him something back. As we learn more about the gift of your son Jesus, help us to give our greatest gifts to you, and to the people you want us to love and care for."

FRIDAY

JESUS CAME AS A SHEPERD TO MAKE A SACRIFICE

Jesus loved us so much that He came to earth and did whatever it took to find His lost people. It's the same kind of sacrifice a shepherd makes to seek for his lost sheep. Jesus still wants to make sacrificial efforts to find the lost; it's part of our job to help Him!

Additional Resources: Small candy canes and hot cocoa

THINGS TO DO:

PUT candy canes on the tree or serve hot cocoa using a small traditional candy cane to stir it. Notice that the candy canes are shaped like a shepherd's staff.

READ Luke 15:8-10. Have you ever lost something and had a really hard time finding it? Tell a story about this.

READ Luke 15:3-7. Consider a few of the sacrifices and efforts a shepherd had to make if he lost a sheep in rugged and dangerous country. How did Jesus make similar sacrifices and efforts to rescue us, just like a good shepherd?

SING "Angels We Have Heard on High," v. 2.

PRAY "Thank you, God, for the Greatest Gift ever given, Jesus your Son. Thank you for Baby Jesus who came and grew up and then made great sacrifices to find and rescue us. As we learn more about the gift of your son Jesus, help us to give our greatest gifts to you, and to the people you want us to love and care for."

SATURDAY

GOD GAVE US GIFTS TO SHARE WITH OTHERS

In response to the coming of King Jesus, the Wise Men came from afar to bring their gifts of adoration to Jesus when He was probably just a toddler. We also have ways we can share gifts and be a gift to others.

Additional Resources: Paper and pen

THINGS TO DO:

READ Matthew 2:11 together. The Magi shared their very special gifts they had when they found the young Jesus.

ASK: Remember or look on line together: what were these gifts used for and why were they so valuable in Jesus' day? Why did they give these valuable gifts to Jesus as a toddler if he could not really use them?

REVIEW Memory Verse: John 3:16 – "For God so loved the world that He gave His only Son that everyone who believes in Him should not perish but have everlasting life."

MAKE an "act of love" coupon for someone outside your family (a neighbor, teacher or friend, e.g.) where you share something of yourself for Christmas: a baked good, a walk, assistance with a difficult chore, etc..

PRAY "Thank you, God, for the Greatest Gift ever given, Jesus your Son. Thank you for Baby Jesus who came and grew up and then made great sacrifices to find and rescue us. As we learn more about the gift of your son Jesus, help us to give our greatest gifts to you, and to the people you want us to love and care for."

WEEK FOUR

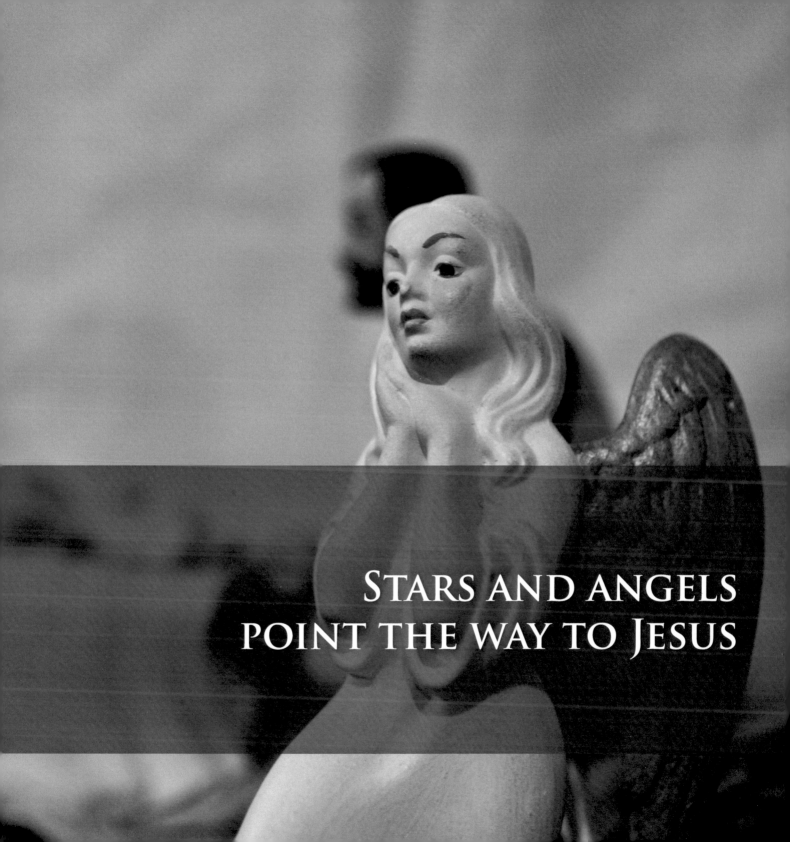

STARS AND ANGELS
POINT THE WAY TO JESUS

THIS WEEK'S EMPHASIS IS

on how God used angels and the star to guide those in the Christmas story. You might want to look at the star or an angel as you read the scriptures or sing the carols.

Christmas symbols to set up: Stars and angels- on tree, Nativity or elsewhere

Additional Resources Needed: Advent wreath and candles, props for acting out the Christmas story, candle(s) , "Rudolf the Red-Nosed Reindeer" or "A Christmas Carol" video.

A Response in your Neighborhood, Community or the World: The week or so after Christmas, decide as a family one way you could point someone you know to Jesus in the year ahead. Make an initial plan of what, when, who, how and then pray together for God's favor.

SUNDAY

STARS AND ANGELS POINT THE WAY TO JESUS

The star and the angels led the Magi and the shepherds to Baby Jesus and His very special birth. The star and angels both remind us that we too sometimes need someone to help us find Jesus, and guide us in our lives.

Additional Resources: Stars and angels to set up, Advent candle, flashlights, Rudolf Christmas video

THINGS TO DO:

SET UP the star and angel(s) on the tree, Nativity or elsewhere in your home.

READ and perhaps act out both Luke 2:8-16 and Matthew 2:1-11 as one continuous story. You can do this as a single houseshold or with one or more families, acting as a procession of Magi and shepherds. Follow both the star and the angels (i.e., parents using flashlights) in order to find Baby Jesus. Use multiple rooms or your local church as your stage. Sing "We Three Kings" v. 1 as you move toward the baby Jesus and act out this story. Pay special attention to the role of the angels and the star.

LIGHT the candle from previous weeks, then lightthe Advent candle. The ***Angels*** or ***Star*** Candle reminds us that we, like the Magi and Christmas characters, receive help in finding God.

REVIEW the Memory Verse, John 8:12-"I am the Light of the world."

PRAY "Thank you, Lord, for sending the star and the angels so that people could find and see the new Baby Jesus. As we celebrate your special birth this week, help us to see and follow everything you show us about how special you are."

WATCH a classic Christmas show, *Rudolf the Red Nosed Reindeer* (Notice how Rudolf's red nose that stormy night acted like the Christmas star did for the Magi and the Shepherds). See the last part of the show-http://www.youtube.com/watch?v=TyTMCsJBvMM)

33

MONDAY

JESUS IS THE BRIGHTEST STAR OF ALL

The star pointed to Jesus when He was a baby. When Jesus grew up, He did not need a star or angels to point to Him. He himself was like the brightest star of all. He was the LIGHT that could guide the whole world.

Additional Resource: Candle

THINGS TO DO:

REVIEW the memory verse: John 8:12-"I am the light of the world."

TURN OUT the lights, then light and hold a candle for the whole family, or one for each family member. Imagine the candle represents Jesus and His light for you.

SHARE a situation where personal or family guidance is needed. Then pray and fill in, "Jesus I need your light to help show me the right way. Help me with _____." Then as a family close together: "Jesus, let your light be our guide."

SING "Silent Night", v. 2 (or the whole song with the candle still burning.)

PRAY "Thank you, Lord, for sending the star and the angels so that people could find and see the new Baby Jesus. As we celebrate your special birth this week, help us to see and follow everything you show us about how special you are."

TUESDAY
EVERYONE NEEDS A STAR

The Magi lived far away from Bethlehem and were from another country and had no cell phones, TV or Internet. They needed to see the star in the sky in order to know about Jesus and then come find him. People who don't know Jesus today need a "human star," someone to show and tell them about Jesus.

Additional Resource: Candle

THINGS TO DO:

READ this short summary of Matthew 2: 1 and 9:"The Magi came to Jerusalem from the East…and there in front of them was the star."

DISCUSS: If the star had not risen in the sky, would the magi have ever found the new King in Bethlehem? How do you think that would have felt?

GO together to another room where you can't see the tree, turn out the lights and light a candle in that room. Remember: People who love Jesus have traveled to faraway places to be a "star" to the people needing help to see Jesus. Take a few minutes to thank God for the people who have helped YOU see Jesus, and then pray for a missionary you know or from your church.

SING "We Three Kings," v. 1 and go back to the living room as you sing.

PRAY "Thank you, Lord, for sending the star and the angels so that people could find and see the new Baby Jesus. As we celebrate your special birth this week, help us to see and follow everything you show us about how special you are."

WEDNESDAY

THE MAGI FOLLOWED THE STAR BY NIGHT

The Magi could only see and follow the star when it was dark outside. And they had no guarantee that they would find what they were looking for. But God gave them the gift of faith that kept them traveling in the dark, confident they would see the new born king. We, too, are to walk by faith.

Additional Resource: Blindfolds

THINGS TO DO:

READ summary of 2 Cor. 5:7-"We walk by faith, not by sight."

HAVE all the family members be blindfolded except the chosen leader who will model Jesus in our lives. Line up in single file, holding the hand or shoulder on the person in front of you. Take a "walk by faith" around the house, trusting your leader and that you won't hit a wall, get hurt, etc. Optional: Sing a Christmas carol as you do the faith walk.

ASK: Sit down by the Christmas tree and ask how that experience of "faith walking" was for each of you. As a parent, suggest how you as a family are walking by faith with Jesus in some area of your life today.

SING "Angels We Have Heard on High," v. 1.

PRAY "Thank you, Lord, for sending the star and the angels so that people could find and see the new Baby Jesus. As we celebrate your special birth this week, help us to see and follow everything you show us about how special you are."

THURSDAY
THE ANGEL POINTED TO THE FUTURE

The stars and angels pointed the people not only to the baby Jesus but also to the future day when "peace on earth and good will to all" would come fully. So every Christmas the angels' message helps us anticipate His Second Coming.

Additional Resource: paper and markers

THINGS TO DO:

ASK: The angels told the Shepherds that this baby Jesus brought good news of peace on earth. Peace means everything and everybody on earth would be perfect and loving, just the way God wanted things to be. Name several things that would be different about the world today if Jesus had already made everything perfect and loving and good.

READ Revelation 22:1-7, the end of the Bible story, using two different readers. Make a short list together of how life in heaven is described. What are a couple similarities you can see between heaven and the Garden of Eden in the creation story?

IMAGINE yourself at Heaven's banquet table as you dress up together, have a Christmas goody on fancy plates together.

SING "Joy to the World," vv. 1, 2 – a description of the world at Christ's Second Coming.

PRAY "Thank you, Lord, for sending the star and the angels so that people could find and see the new Baby Jesus. As we celebrate your special birth this week, help us to see and follow everything you show us about how special you are."

FRIDAY

THE STAR POINTED TO A GREATER CHRISTMAS

The worship of the magi, the joy of the shepherds, and the obedience of Mary will all be much greater in heaven. May the first Christmas story and our family's life together point our hearts to the future coming of Jesus.

THINGS TO DO:

DO a short family Christmas chore or activity of your choice (cleaning, wrapping, decorating, writing out a card, etc.) and sing a Christmas song as you do, to help you remember why you are doing what you are doing: we are getting ready for the second coming of Jesus.

READ Isaiah 60: 1, 3, 6- This is the description of what other kings and magi in the world will do when Christ comes to earth the second time.

SING "Joy to the World," v. 3 – listen for the description of the world at Christ's Second Coming.

REVIEW the Memory Verse: John 8:12-"I am the Light of the world."

PRAY "Thank you, Lord, for sending the star and the angels so that people could find and see the new Baby Jesus. As we celebrate your special birth this week, help us to see and follow everything you show us about how special you are."

CHRISTMAS EVE
THE WAITING IS OVER, JESUS IS HERE!

THINGS TO DO:

LIGHT the Advent candles and the middle one: the Christmas candle.

UNWRAP Baby Jesus and put him in the Nativity set or you can do this Christmas morning before you open your other gifts.

READ the story, "If He Had Not Come," our family's most treasured Christmas story (find this online).

ADVENT AS A TIME TO PREPARE AND REMEMBER

The church's historic observance of Advent and her twin sister Lent were created in the same spirit of God's unwavering intent for Israel, His people: they were to forever celebrate feasts and holidays as a way to remember their God and their identity as His chosen vessel and bride. Unlike my own North American heritage, with its melting pot and accommodating culture, the Jews were committed to remain a people set aside and holy from the nations around them. If there had been no Sabbath with its mandated rest, no Passover feast with its rich symbols, no feasts with the gathered community to hear again the stories, then the Jews would have quickly assimilated into the surrounding culture. They would have quietly dissolved as God's people and become simply another casualty of history. But in telling and retelling the central stories of their faith, Jewish parents passed down to the next generation the foundations upon which to build their future lives in a foreign land. For in remembering, the Jews believed the past became in a real sense, present again to help shape their future. The God of these stories told is here with us now, they believe, on the stage and backdrop of the ongoing drama of God in their homes, neighborhoods and everyday life.

Remembering and building traditions has always been serious business. It still is. How do God's people remember and stay true to Christ in a culture where our loyalties are lured powerfully to a host of distractions and dead ends? How do we parent kids today in a way they stay true to the faith in Christ we seek to pass on?

The Lewises don't have easy answers here, but there are ancient practices to rediscover and modify in our own day. Advent is one such season to experiment and develop life long holiday memories. Perhaps our thirst for something more at the holidays is affirming the importance of creating Christmas traditions with our family.

The tradition of Advent is in its essence a period of preparation for something too important to approach quickly or lightly. What the season of engagement was to my wedding, what the months of planning were to our family's month long cross country trip, so Advent is to Christmas. Our four weeks of preparation will likely be inseparable from – and perhaps as meaningful as – Christmas Day itself.

We are invited by God during Advent to set aside an extended time beforehand to cultivate traditions, traditions that both anticipate the holiday temptations and give us more space to become attentive to Jesus Christ.

As the carol rings: "let every heart, prepare him room."

MORE ON THE THREE DISTINCT HOPES OF THIS BOOK

Over the years, as my family's Christmas traditions emerged, my wife and I worked identified hopes for our children's experience of Christmas. These hopes-or goals-help provide a framework for how we celebrated Advent and helped us create the impetus for creating this book.

Throughout the Christmas season, our hopes are:

To appreciate more deeply the connections of the Christmas story with the Christmas symbols.

Many of my warmest childhood memories of Christmas are connected to its symbols: cutting our tree, hanging ornaments, putting up the lights and the star, and opening my stocking and gifts. But I was never shown how these symbols, with the exception of the star and the manger scene, could help me better understand meaning of Christmas. At church I would hear and sing about the Bethlehem birth story, but the presents and stockings, trees and lights, all the symbols I loved, I never knew what they had to do with the coming of God into the world as one of us. This created for me an unfortunate disconnect. The same was true for Carissa.

When our first children arrived, it was our strong desire that they would see the beauty of Jesus' birth story throughout the season. We hoped to eliminate our own disconnect from their experience. So we set out to reconnect trees and lights and stockings and packages to the Christ and the Christmas story. Along the way, we discovered that the majority of these traditional symbols and practices either originally had strong Christian roots that could be reclaimed, or that these treasured symbols could be easily infused with new meaning through the lens of the Bethlehem birth.

To have the Christmas season provide an annual revisiting of key foundations of our Christian faith.

As our children began to grow up, we made a second discovery: looking more deeply at these Christmas symbols during the four weeks of Advent seemed a fantastic way not only to revisit the Bethlehem story but also the fundamentals of our entire Christian faith. This Advent experience in our family has become a significant and annual piece of preparing them to know and own their faith in Christ. As parents we knew we wanted to help ground them in the basics, but we seemed to lack the tools and resources, and the discipline and time to do it. After several Christmases, we decided that Advent would be our extended time period to repeatedly expose them to these fundamentals. This contents of this book have been our guide, Christmas after Christmas.

Drawing from existing Christmas symbols and the resources of others, I have sought to develop a fun and intentional approach to helping our family have an annual place to learn, digest, and revisit the basic Bible story. The book serves as an informal catechism in introducing the foundations of our life of faith with Jesus Christ, the church, and the world.

To let these traditions, practiced in the busy and full Christmas holiday season, prepare us for a lifetime of making faith commitments in a "foreign land".

Early on in our parenting, Carissa and I chose to be bold in our family's remembrance of God and in the faith training of our children. We made the commitment to offer Advent as our first fruits of the Christian year. As flexible and fun as Carissa and I have tried to make our Advent traditions, nothing took place without some priority-making, planning, and protecting. We had to say no a few times early on to genuinely good holiday expectations and possibilities. Otherwise, with all these new Advent activities added, our family ship would have sunk in overload. And while Christmas for us is, of course, a full and active time, we experimented early on to find a flexible way of celebrating that has not felt overwhelming or disjointed. Our regrets are fewer than our life-long memories. We have stumbled forward in the messiness and wonder of the season each year, and have seen how He leads our family into an annual rediscovery of the treasure of Christmas, and how He helps us to better live in that treasure all year long.

ANGELS WE HAVE HEARD ON HIGH

Angels we have on heard high
Sweetly singing ore the plains
And the mountains in reply
Echoing their joyous strains

Chorus: Gloria in excelsis Deo
Gloria in excelsis Deo

Come to Bethlehem and see
Christ whose birth the angels sing
Come adore on bended knee
Christ the Lord the newborn King

Chorus

AWAY IN A MANGER

Away in a manger, no crib for a bed
The little Lord Jesus lay down His sweet head
The stars in the sky looked down where
He lay
The little Lord Jesus asleep on the hay

The cattle are lowing, the Baby awakes
But little Lord Jesus, no crying He makes
I love Thee, Lord Jesus, look down from
the sky
And stay by my cradle 'til morning is nigh

HARK THE HERALD ANGELS SING

Hark! The herald angels sing,
Glory to the newborn King,
Peace on earth and mercy mild
God and sinners reconciled.

Joyful all ye nations rise
Join the triumph of the skies
With angelic host proclaim
Christ is born in Bethlehem
Hark! The herald angels sing,
"Glory to the newborn King."

JOY TO THE WORLD

Joy to the world! The Lord is come:
let earth receive him King!
Let every heart prepare him room
and heaven and nature sing. (Repeat)

Joy to the world! the Saviour reigns:
let men their songs employ
while fields and floods rocks hills
and plains
repeat the sounding joy. (Repeat)

He rules the earth with truth and grace,
and makes the nations prove
the glories of his righteousness
and wonders of his love. (Repeat)

O COME, ALL YE FAITHFUL

O come, all ye faithful,
Joyful and triumphant;
O come ye, O come ye to Bethlehem.
Come and behold Him,
Born the King of angels;

Chorus:
O come, let us adore Him;
O come, let us adore Him;
O come, let us adore Him,
Christ the Lord!